THE CATECHISM OF INDIAN MUSIC

WITH SONGS

THE CATECHISM OF INDIAN MUSIC

WITH SONGS

MUTTY LALL SEAL

GYAN

Published by

Gyan Publishing House
5, Ansari Road
Daryaganj, New Delhi-110002
Phone: 011-47034999, 9811692060
E-mail: books@gyanbooks.com

Distribution Network
gyanbooks.com
India, USA, Canada, UK, Australia

ISBN: 978-93-7169-339-4 (PB)

First Published, 1893

2nd Impression 2025

Printed at: Gyan Press, Delhi.

THE CATECHISM OF INDIAN MUSIC WITH SONGS
Author: MUTTY LALL SEAL

THE

CATECHISM OF INDIAN MUSIC

WITH SONGS,

BY

MOHINDRO LALL SEAL,

Honorary Member of the Managing Committee,

BENGAL MUSIC SCHOOL,

AUTHOR OF THE

"INDEX OF KANTHA-KAÚMUDI"

OF 1877.

AND OF

"THE MUSICAL CHART"—1885.

1893.

DEDICATION.

To His Highness

THE RAJAH SIR SOURINDRO MOHUN TAGORE,

DOCTOR OF MUSIC,

Founder and President, Bengal Academy of Music,

&c., *&c.,* *&c.*

Your Highness,

WHILE dedicating this little book, I beg most humbly to submit that I, for a long time studied and practised Hindu Music with care and diligence in the Bengal Music School, and that the Catechism, I have the honor to place into Your Highness' hands, embodies the notes on theoretical and practical music, which I could then collect, and other invaluable informations on the subject, with which I was favored by Your Highness. I consider a book on Hindu Music, similar in scope to this "Catechism," a *desideratum*, and believe that the students of this branch of learning, will derive some help from it in undergoing their annual examinations.

If Your Highness will look upon it with a sympathetic eye, I shall consider my labors amply repaid.

I have the honor to be,
Your Highness'
Most obedient Student of Music,
MOHINDRO LALL SEAL.

INTRODUCTION.

IN submitting this small book, entitled "The Catechism of Indian Music with Songs," in English, for the perusal of such persons as take some interest in the subject, the Author craves leave to state that, the original was, some time ago, written in Bengali for gratuitous circulation among his fellow Musicians, and the Teachers and Managers of Institutions in this City and other places in Bengal, where Hindu Music is regularly and systematically taught, and where earnest steps are being taken for the cultivation and propagation of this interesting Art. The Bengali edition has been presented to several Europeans of distinguished position, Maharajahs, Rajahs and other Noblemen, and to many Bengali Gentlemen, who were expected to appreciate its contents and pass their opinion thereon. The Author has lately been advised by Monsier J. Jouslain, Consul-General for France in Calcutta, to translate the small book into English, in order that the subject matter of it, may receive the attention of the *Savants* of Europe and America.

Acting up to this valuable suggestion, the Author has edited the book, which he now has the honor of placing before the public. He has herein done his best to present an exposition of the principles and varied technicalities of Indian Music, with such accuracy and intelligibility, as his knowledge and command of the English language, would enable him to do ; and he hopes and trusts that the imperfections that will necessarily be found in the publication, will be generously excused. He has spent several years of his life in the study of Indian Music, and in the congenial task of diffusing a knowledge of it among his fellow-beings ; any hints or suggestions, therefore, for the improvement of the present treatise, will be most gratefully received and readily utilized in future editions of it.

M. L. SEAL.

131., AMHERST STREET.
Calcutta, 29th November 1895.

INDEX.

THEORETICAL MUSIC.

AUPAPATTIKA TAURYATRIKA

OR

THEORETICAL MUSIC.

THE

Catechism of Hindu Music.

CHAPTER I.

AUPAPATTIKA TAURYATRIKA,

OR

THEORETICAL MUSIC.

---:o:---

Q.—What is called *Sangíta Sástrá*?

A.—The science that teaches us how to sing, play on instruments and to dance, is called *Sangíta Sástra.*

Q.—Into how many parts is *Sangíta Sástra* divided?

A.—*Sangíta Sástra* is divided into three parts; namely, *Gíta* (song), *Vádya* (playing on instruments) and *Nritya* (dancing).

Q.—What is the technical term for the union of the three?

A—*Tauryatrika.*

Q.—Into how many portions is *Tauryatrika* classified?

A.—Two; namely, *Aupapattika* (Theoretical) and *Kriyásiddha* (Practical).

Q.—What is the literal signification of the terms *Aupapattika* and *Kriyásiddha*?

A.—The work that treats of and defines the laws and principles of Music is called *Aupapattika Tauryatrika*, and that which gives the rules and practical directions for singing, dancing and performances upon Musical instruments is called *Kriyásiddha Tauryatrika*.

Q.—Into how many sections is *Sangíta* divided?

A.—Two; namely, *Visible* and *Audible*. *Visible Sangíta* embraces *Nritya* (dance) and dramatic exhibitions, and *Audible Sangíta* is represented by vocal and instrumental Music.

Q.—What is called *Nritya*?

A.—*Nritya* is a succession of movements of hands, feet and other members of the body up and down, backwards and forwards, expressive of lascivious emotions, regulated by the rules of metre and accompanied by the sound of instruments; or in other words, it is a movement of one's body in measured steps, to a musical accompaniment, either singly or in company with others.

Q.—With how many *Rasas* (sentiments) is dance connected?

A.—Five; namely, *Víra* (courage or heroism), *Sringára* (love), *Bhayánaka* (fear), *Hásya* (laughter) and *Ascharya* (wonder).

Q.—What is called *Gíta* (song) and into how many parts is it divided ?

A.—There are two kinds of *Gíta* (song); *Vocal* and *Instrumental*. The unspeakably melodious sound which is uttered by means of the seven notes in conjunction with time is called the *Vocal Song* (or *Kantha-Gíta*), while the expression of the seven notes on instruments, according to defined time, is called the Instrumental Song (or *Yantra Gíta*).

Q.—Into how many parts is *Sangíta* divided according to usage ?

A.—Two; namely, *Márga* and *Desí*.

Q.—What is called *Márga-Sangíta* ?

A.—The style of *Sangíta* which Brahmá, Bharata and the other *Rishis* sang before Mahádeva is called *Márga-Sangíta*.

Q.—What is the *Desí-Sangíta* ?

A.—*Desí* (or local) *Sangíta* has its origin in the manners, habits and character of the people with whom it prevails.

Q.—What are the essential parts of *Gíta* and its requisites ?

A.—*Dhátu* (Notes) and *Mátrá* (Time) are the essential parts of *Gíta*. Its principal requisites are *Tála* (measure), *Rága* and *Ráginí*; (which is the off-shoot of the *Rága*).

Q.—How many kinds of *Kantha-Gíta* (Vocal Music) are there ?

A.—Several; among these are *Swaragráma* (from *Swara,* musical sound and *Gráma,* collection, *i. e.,* a series of notes arranged according to Musical laws), *Telená, Kheyál, Chaturanga, Tribat, Bishnupad, Tapkheyál, Dhrupad, Játa, Káwal, Gulnaks, Rágamálá, Álápa, Tappá;* &c., &c. There is no necessity for a regular *tála* in the rendering of a *Rága* by means of the *Álápa* (which is done by various modulations, such as the *múrchchhaná* and *tána*).

Q.—What is called *Rága* and what is the difference between *Rága* and *Gíta* ?

A.—"*Ranjayati Rága,*" as defined by *Bharata.* That which pleases is a *Rága.* The arrangement of musical notes according to given rules with *Mátrá* (time) and *Múrchchhaná* (the gliding of a note into another, in a scale of ascension and descension, without an intermediate interruption of the *Srutis* with the various resultant vibrations) constitutes the *Rága.* The *Rága* does not require *tála* (a defined measure) but *Gíta* does.

Q.—What are the names and characteristics of the *Swaras* with reference to the composition of a *Rága* ?

A.—*Vádi, Samvádi, Anuvádi* and *Vivádi.* The principal note that produces the *Rága* and determines its particular character, and is frequently used in it, is called *Vádi; Samvádi* helps *Vádi* in expressing the character of a *Rága*, but is only second to the *Vádi* in the frequency of its use ; *Anuvádi* comes the third in the order of its use and facilitates the completion of a *Rága*; the *Vivádi* destroys the character of a *Rága* and is never admissible in it.

Illustrations.

	Vádi.	*Samvádi.*	*Vivádi.*
Bhairav	$\overset{\triangle}{\text{ri}}$ ($\overset{\triangle}{\text{D}}$)	ga (E), $\overset{\triangle}{\text{dha}}$ ($\overset{\triangle}{\text{A}}$)	Nil
Bhairavi	$\overset{\triangle}{\text{dha}}$ ($\overset{\triangle}{\text{A}}$)	$\overset{\triangle}{\text{ga}}$ ($\overset{\triangle}{\text{E}}$)	,,
Rámkelí	ma (F)	$\overset{\triangle}{\text{ri}}$ ($\overset{\triangle}{\text{D}}$), $\overset{\triangle}{\text{dha}}$ ($\overset{\triangle}{\text{A}}$)	,,
Yogiṉá	ma (F)	$\overset{\triangle}{\text{ri}}$ ($\overset{\triangle}{\text{D}}$), $\overset{\triangle}{\text{dha}}$ ($\overset{\triangle}{\text{A}}$)	,,
Bibhásha	dha (A)	ga (E)	ma (F)
Àláhiyá	dha (A)	ga (E)	Nil
Sarfordá	ga (E)	ma (F)	,,
Sindhu	ma (F)	$\overset{\triangle}{\text{ga}}$ ($\overset{\triangle}{\text{E}}$)	,,
Torí	$\overset{\triangle}{\text{dha}}$ ($\overset{\triangle}{\text{A}}$)	ga (E)	,,
Vrindávani-Sáraṉga	ri (D)	ni (B)	ga (E), dha (A)
Multáni	$\overset{\triangle}{\text{ga}}$ ($\overset{\triangle}{\text{E}}$)	$\overset{\triangle}{\text{dha}}$ ($\overset{\triangle}{\text{A}}$)	Nil
Hámvira	dha (A)	ga (E)	,,
Bhupálí	ga (E)	dha (A)	,,
Iman-Kalyán	pa (G)	ga (E)	,,

	Vádi.	*Samvádi.*	*Vivádi.*
Kánará	ga (E) with (∆) sign	dha (A) with (∆) sign	Nil
Vágíswarí	ni (B)	ga (E), ma (F)	„
Khámbáj	ga (E)	ma (F)	„
Jhinjhití	ga (E)	ma (F), pa (G)	„
Behág	ga (E)	ni (B)	„
Báhár	ma (F)	ga (E)	„

N. B.—The sign (∆) is for *Komala swaras* or flats, (∆̱) is for *ati Komala swaras* or the *very* flats.

Q.—What is the difference between one *Rága* or *Rágini* and another?

A.—The difference lies in the ascending and descending order of succession of the notes with reference to the *Vádi, Samvádi* and *Anuvádi* and in the determination of the *Vivádi.*

Q.—How does *Bibhásha* differ from *Bhupáli*?

A.—In *Bibhásha dha* (A) is the *Vádi, ga* (E) is the *Samvádi* and *ma* (F) is the *Vivádi.* It moves thus;—From *pa* (G) and *dha* (A) of the *Mudárá Septime* to *ri* (D) and *sá* (C) of *Tárá;* again from *sá* (C) of the *Mudárá* with *dha* (A) of the *Udárá* and *ri* (D) of the *Mudárá* to *sá* (C) where it rests. It descends thus:—From *sá* (C) of the *Tárá* to *ni* (B), *dha* (A) and *pa* (G) and then to *ga* (E), *ri* (D) and *sá* (C) of the *Mudárá.* As regards *Bhupáli*:—It has its *Vádi* in *ga* (E) and *Samvádi* in *dha* (A). It moves from *ga* (E) to *pa* (G) and back at once to *ri* (D) of the *Mudárá*. Again, from *sá* (C) of the *Tárá* to *dha* (A) of *Mudárá* and then to *ri* (D) of the *Tárá*. It descends thus :—From *sá* (C) of the *Tárá* to *dha* (A) and *pa* (G) and then to *ga* (E) to *ri* (D) and *sá* (C) of the *Mudárá* where it rests.

Q.—In how many ways are the *Rágas* formed, and what are they called ?

A.—Four :—1. *Árohana* and *Abarohana rúpa*, *i.e.*, notes in their ascending and descending series.

2. *Vikrita rúpa*; *i. e.*, Artificial notes (the formation of other notes from the 7 original notes ; the 12 *Vikritas*).

3. *Múrchchhaná rúpa.*

4. *Grámik rúpa ; i. e.*, serial arrangement of notes according to given rules.

MÚRCHCHHANA RÚPA.

(Gliding of a note into another in the scale of ascension and descension).

Q.—How is the word *Múrchchhaná* derived and what is its meaning ?

A.—As nature undergoes a change, having lost its original simplicity and assumes different aspects, so *Suddha Swaras* (the original or natural notes), suffer a change, losing their fundamental sounds and form into several *Swaras* or tones. Hence the changes in the character of *Swaras* and *Anuswaras* (semitones) are called the *Múrchchhanás*; or, in short, *Múrchchhaná* means the conversion of the *Suddha Swaras* (natural tones) and *Anuswaras* into other shapes.

Q.—How many *Swaras* and *Anuswaras* can there be, having regard to their *Komalatá* (flatness), *Tívratá*, (sharpness) and *Grámikatá* (disposition) ?

A.—In each *Gráma* (a series of notes) there are seven *Suddha Swaras* (7 original notes), hence there are seven *Múrchchhita Swaras* in each *Gráma*, and so in three *Grámas* there are 21 *Múrchchhita Múla Swaras* (fundamental notes).

As regards flats and sharps, excepting the Sharja (C the tonick) and the fifth note (G), both of which are fix tones, the other 5 notes have each a transformation ; for this reason in each *Gráma* there are 12 *Prakrita Swaras* (Diatonic notes) and *Vikrita Swaras* (Chromatic notes) ; and in 3 *Grámas* there are 36 *Swaras* and 36 *Múrchchhanás*. Again, owing to the different gradations of the flats and sharps, each *Swara* in possessed of a *Saptakut-Múrchchhaná*. Generally the *Múrchchhanás* of the *Prakrita* (natural) and *Vikrita* (artificial) tones are perceptible and recognised. But only such persons as have got the divine gift to understand the *minutæ* of *Swaras* and have the ability to express them, can understand and perform *Kút-Múrchchhanás.*

Q.—What is the use of the *Múrchchhanás* ?

A.—The *Múrchchhanás* are the ornaments of *Rágas* and serve to differentiate them from one another, by means of the order of their operation. Thus, where two *Rágas* are each composed on a scale of seven full notes, one may be quite distinct from the other; because, for instance, the notes D and A may be under *Múrchchhaná* in the case of the one, and E and B in that of the other.

GRÁMIKA RÚPA.

(Serial arrangement of Notes according to laws).

Q.—How many *Kúts* are mentioned in the *Sangíta Sástra* (Musical Science) ?

A.—Forty-nine.

Q.—What is the meaning of the word *Kút* ?

A.—The *Grámik Swara* (*Swara* or note as arranged according to the musical laws) with its *Anúswara* is called *Kút.*

Q.—How many *Anúswaras* are there in each *Grámikaswara* ?

A.—Six.

Q.—Into how many classes are the *Anúswaras* divided?

A.—Two.

Q.—What constitutes the two classes of *Anúswaras*?

A.—The Flats and the Sharps.

Q.—With reference to the *Sahajatá* (naturalness), *Tívratá* (sharpness) and *Komalatá* (flatness) of the *Swaras*, there should be three classes of *Swaras* and A*núswras* in the *Kút*, and so there should be in all 21 *Kúts* in a *Gráma*; but how is it that its total number is 49?

A.—There are six degrees of *Komlatá* (flatness) and *Tívratá* (sharpness) of A*núswara*; *viz*; *Komala* (flat), *Komalatara* (flatter), *Komalatama* (flattest); and *Tívra* (sharp), *Tívratara* (sharper) and *Tívratama* (sharpest). Hence a *Swara* (fundamental note) together with its *Six Anúswaras*, makes 7 *Kúts*; and when each of the seven fundamental notes is thus treated, the total comes to 49 *Kúts*.

Q.—What do you know about the *Graha*, the *Añsa* and the *Nyása*?

A.—The *Añsa* implies the *Vádi*. The classical Authorities have laid down that the *Rága* should begin with the *Graha* and stop at the *Nyása* note, these notes being the same as the *Vádi* (leading note, explained before). But according to modern practice, the Composer determines the note, with which the *Rága* should begin. A little consideration will show that it would be better to place the *Graha* on the *Vádi*, *i. e.*, to begin a *Rága* with the leading note, for then its character would unfold itself at once; or at least to begin a *Rága* with the *Samvádi* note (which is the next highest to the *Vádi* in the order of its frequency). It would also be better to fix *Sharja* (C) as the *Samápaka-swara* or the *Nyása* (terminal note) for all the *Rágas*, as several Authorities have done. In certain songs, however, a contrary usage is observed. In fact, the laws of *Graha* and *Nyása* apply more strictly to the *Álápa* than to the song.

Q.—Into how many species are the *Rágas* and *Rágineeṡ* divided, and how are these again classified?

A.—There are three species, *viz.*, *Suddha* (*i.e.* pure, self-existing), *Sálañka*, (a compound of two *Rágas*) and *Sañkírna* (a compound of three or more). Each of these species is again sub-divided into three classes, *viz.*, *Orava* (composed of five notes), *Khárava* (composed of six notes) and *Sampúrna* (composed of seven notes).

Q.—What are the *Alañkáras* (ornaments of *Gán*, song) ?

A.—*Tána* (*Tána* is formed from *Murchchhanás*, it means, the extension of a melody by way of ascension or descension); *Báñt* (the singing or performing a portion of a *Rága*, now in the *Uchha-saptaka* (highest septime), now in the *Nimna-saptaka*, (lowest septime) and then in the *Madhya-saptaka* (middle septime); *Dama* (singing a portion in one continuous stream of time from commencement to end); *Lágdáñt* (continuation of the notes in singing or playing, without causing a pause or a break in the *Srutis* (the minutest particles of sound that can be perceived by the ear) and *Kartava* (singing or performing short *ad-libitum* passages consistent with the character of the *Rága*, that is being rendered); without these ornaments, *Gán* (song) and *Vádya* (instrumental music) become dull and vapid and lose all zest.

Q.—What is the number of the actions of the organism of the throat with reference to singing?

A.—Three, namely; *Gamaka* (shake: when the air in the lungs being expanded with internal heat escapes, forcing its way out through the wind-pipe, it causes a vibration of the guttural chords and thereby produces on the notes what is called the *Gamak)*; *Múrchchhanás* and *Khudra Tániká* (short *Tánas)* or *Gítkári* (which is a peculiar modulation of the voice over a certain note or a series of notes, giving them a tremulous sound; but not to such an extent as would render the note or notes operated upon, inadmissible in the *Rága* that is being rendered).

CHAPTER II.

NÁDA, SRUTI AND SWARA.

—:o:—

Q.—What is called the *Náda*?

A.—*Náda* is derived from the root *Nada*, which means sound. The sound which, produced by a vibratory motion, forms the basis of *Saptaswaras* or fundamental seven musical notes is called *Náda*; or in other words, *Náda* is that sound which produces the seven notes.

"*Naddbhyân játátvát nádah.*"

That which is derived from *na* and *da* is called *Náda.*

"*Nakárah pránabáyuh syát,*
Dakáro habyabáhanah;
Tábhyañ sañjáyate jasmát,
Tasmát náda iti Smritah."

The air, (the breath of life) while in the lungs during respiration, is compressed and heated up with the internal heat (animal heat) and assumes a motive, volitive and expansive motion, resulting in a sudden concussion or agitation, and while escaping through the wind-pipe, it vibrates the passage, and thus various tones of the human voice are produced, which are called *Nádas.* The inhaled air coming in contact with electricity, is repulsed towards the navel and escapes from the throat, vibrating the chords in the larynx. The effect of the phenomenon is called *Náda.*

Q.—How is the *Náda* produced and how is it rendered audible ?

A.—According to the *Sanskrita* Authorities, *Náda* is produced from *Byom* or ether, one of the five self-existing elements that pervade the Universe. These elements are called *Kshiti* (earth), *Ap* (water), *Teja* (fire), *Marut* (air) and *Byom* (ether). The sound which is produced from the concussion of material substances, mixes with the air and is, in its motion, drifted into the human ear, where beating against the tympanum or the drum of the ear, gives rise to a sensation which is felt in the brains. The effect of the atmospheric vibrations on the membrane is called *Náda.*

Q.—What is the nature of the *Náda* and how do *Náda,* the *Sruti* and the *Swara* stand in relation to one another ?

A.—*Náda* admits of no ascension or descension. It represents an even tenour of sound. But when the particles of sound, rise or fall, then they come to be called *Dhvani* (sound). The subtle parts of sound are called *Sruti* (which means that which can be perceived by the ear) and the gross parts are called *Swara* (note). The minute notes that exist between one note and another are the *Srutis.* According to the ancient Musicians, the *Sruti* produces the *Swara.* There are 22 *Srutis* in all. To understand them practically, a couple of *Vinás* are required, each being furnished with 22 chords. The first chord should be tuned so low, that if it is lowered further, no sound may be perceived by the ear; the second chord should be tuned higher than the first, so that no perceivable note may exist between the two; and so on with the remaining chords. The sound produced by the first chord is called the first *Sruti*; that by the second, the second *Sruti,* and so on to the 22nd chord, which represents the 22nd *Sruti.* The fourth chord will produce *Sharja Swara* (C), the seventh the *Rishava* (D), the nineth *Gándhára* (E), the thirteenth *Madhyama* (F), the seventeenth *Panchama* (G), the twentieth *Dhaivata* (A) and the twenty-second *Nishâda Swara* (B): supposing each dot to represent a *Sruti*, the following table represents a *Swaragráma* or scale :—

Sá	Ri	Ga	Ma	Pa	Dha	Ni
C	D	E	F	G	A	B

Modern Musicians, however, draw out the scale, in just the opposite way, thus :—

Sá	Ri	Ga	Ma	Pa	Dha	Ni
C	D	E	F	G	A	B

If the *Sáriká* (frets) of *Viná* and other instruments are observed carefully, the opinion of the modern Musicians will appear more reasonable, because the arrangement of the frets in the instruments, exactly accords with the intervals that exist between the notes, with reference to the intervening *Srutis*.

Q.—How is the *Náda* divided?

A.—There are two kinds of *Náda*; the *Varnátmaka* (articulate) and the *Dhvanwátmaka* (inarticulate).

Q.—What are called the articulate and the inarticulate sounds?

A.—The sound which is produced by means of the nose, throat, head, palate and the teeth is called the articulate sound, and that which is produced by means of striking one thing on another is called the inarticulate sound.

Q.—Into how many parts have the Musicians divided each of these two sounds?

A.—Two; namely, the accordant and the discordant.

Q.—What is the difference between the accordant and the discordant sound?

A.—The sound which is produced in given time by the impulse or progressive vibration of a material substance, or which, on account of its soothing and attractive properties, is worthy of being rendered by the human voice, is called the accordant sound. All others are called the discordant sounds, these are not produced by any limited number of vibrations, nor are they subject to the rules of harmonic progression.

Q.—Illustrate the nature of the *Svara* (note)?

A.—As the horse can naturally run and yet man can direct its motion according to his wishes; so every human being can control the Music that is inherent in his voice, and bring it to the use required.

Q.—How far does sound travel naturally in the air?

A.—When the atmosphere is normal, *i. e.*, when it is neither intensely hot nor cold, nor surcharged with dews, sound travels about 3,400 cubits in a second.

Q.—What are the names of the twenty-two *Srutis?*

A.—*Tívrá, Kumudvati, Mandá, Chchhandavatí, Dayávatí, Ranjaní Ratiká, Raudrí, Krodhí, Vajriká, Prasáriní, Príti, Márjjaní, Kshiti, Raktá, Sandípaní, Álápaní, Mandantí, Rohiní, Ramyá, Ugrá and Kshobhiní.*

Q.—According to the disposition of the *Srútis* in a scale of seven notes, the order is 4, 3, 2, 4, 4, 3, 2; why they cannot be disposed in the order of 3, 2, 4, &c.?

A.—Because that is their natural disposition.

Q.—How can the law of placing the *Sruti* on *Prakrita* (natural) notes or *Vikrita* (chromatic) notes be determined?

A.—Even Bramhá himself could not determine it.

"*Srúti Sthâne Swarañ baktuñ*
Nálañ Bramhápi Sakyate."

i. e., Bramha even could not determine the position of the *Srutis* in the *Svaras.*

"*Julecha Sutaráñ margo minánáñ*
Nopa lakshyate gagane pakshináñ yadvat
Tadvat Swaragatá Sruti."

i. e., As in the case of the fish swimming in the waters or of the birds flying in the air, the passage of the *Srutis* between the notes cannot be traced.

Q.—How is the *Svara* produced?

A.—It is produced from the *Sruti.*

Q.—How many *Svaras* are there in all?

A.—Seven ; *viz. :—Sharja* (C), *Rishabha* (D), *Gándhára* (E), *Madhyama* (F), *Panchama* (G), *Dhaivata* (A) *and Nishdda* (B). Their initials are respectively, *Sá, Ri, Ga, Ma, Pa, Dha* and *Ni.*

Q.—What is *Svara* called in ordinary conversation ?

A.—In language other than that of Science or Art, *Svara* is called *Súr*.

Q.—What *Suras* become *Vikrita* (chromatic) and what are their signs ?

A.—*Ri* (D), *Ga* (E), *Ma* (F), *Dha* (A) and *Ni* (B).

Sámánya-Komal (slightly flat) ... ... △̊

Madhya-Komal (neither slightly flat nor very flat) ... ... △

Ati-Komal (very flat) ... ... △̊

Sámánya-tivra (slightly sharp) ... ... ᚁ

Madhya-tivra (neither slightly sharp nor very sharp) ... ... ᚁ

Ati-tivra (very sharp) ... ... ᚁ̊

Q.—Are the terms *Kari* aud *Tivra* the same ?

A.—*Kari* is the Hindi for the Sanskrit term *Tivra.*

Q.—How are the names of the seven *Suras* derived ?

A.—The *Sura* or Note from which the other six *Suras* are formed, is called *Sharja.* The *Rigveda* used to be chanted in *Rishabha,* hence the term *Rishabha. Gándhára* is derived from the *Gandharbhas* (celestial Musicians).

The *Sura* that is placed in the middle of the Septime, is called *Madhyama* or middle note. *Panchama* is so called because the note counts *Pancham* (fifth), beginning from *Sà* in the Septime. The *Sura* that bears an affinity to the other *Suras* is called *Dhaivata*. *Nisháda* is so called because it is the last in the Septime. Again, each of the seven notes is presided over by a Deity, thus :—

Sharja is presided over by *Agni* (the God of Fire).

Rishabha by *Bramhá* (the Creator).

Gándhára by *Saraswati* (the Goddess of Learning and Music).

Madhyama by *Mahádeva* (the Destroyer).

Panchama by *Náráyana* (the Preserver).

Dhaivata by *Ganesa* (the God of Success).

Nisháda by *Surya* (the Sun).

Each of the seven notes is taken from an animal or a bird :—

Sharja is derived from the call of the Peacock.

Rishabha from the bellow of the Ox.

Gándhára from the bleating of the Goat.

Madhyama from the howling of the Jackal.

Panchama from the song of the black bird, called in Sañskrita, *Kokila*.

Dhaivata from the neigh of the Horse.

Nishháda from the cry of the Elephant.

Q.—What are the numbers of *Prakrita* and *Vikrita Svaras* (natural and chromatic notes) ?

A.—When *Svaras* are in their natural state, they are seven; but when they are transformed into flats and sharps, they are twelve.

Q.—How is *Sharja* defined in the Sañskrit-texts ?

"*Shat jáyante Yasmát.*"

That from which *Rishabha* and the five other *Suras* are derived is called *Sharja*.

—:o:—

CHAPTER III.

MÁTRÁ, LAYA, TÁLA AND CHHANDAH.

Q.—What are *Mátrás* and how many are they in number ?

A.—The word *Mátrá* means time, space or duration. If the unmeasurable and infinite "Time" is divided into small portions, each of such portions is called a *Mátrá*. Such portion or quantity of time as is taken to pronounce a vowel sound is called a *Mátrá*. The *Mátrás* are five in number, *viz.*, *Hrasva* (the duration of time representing the pronunciation of a short vowel); *Dírgha* (that representing the pronunciation of a long vowel); *Plúta* (the time taken to pronounce three or more short vowels); *Ardha* and

Anu representing respectively half and one-fourth of the time a short vowel takes to pronounce.

Q.—What are the signs of the five *Mátrás* and how are they placed?

A.—(|) Represents the duration of *Hrasva Mátrá* (one short vowel sound); (‖) represents the duration of *Dírgha Mátrá* (one long vowel sound); (◡̇) (*Ardha-Chandra* or crescent) represents *Ardha Mátrá* (one-half of a short vowel sound); (×) (*Damaru* or cross) represents *Anu Mátrá* (one-quarter of a short vowel sound). These signs are always placed upon the notes, the *Plúta Mátrá* is represented by three or more of the perpendicular bars, as the case may be. The *Plúta* time is used in calling at a distance, or in crying or singing.

Q.—What are the opinions of the *Sañskrita* Grammarians and Musicians with regard to the *Mátrás*?

A.—As the seven notes; *Sá, Ri, Ga, Ma, Pa, Dha,* and *Ni,* (constituting the Septime) form the essence of Music, so the five *Mátrás,* (*Hrasva, Dírgha, Plúta, Ardha* and *Anu*), form the essence of Measure. According to the Grammarians, the division of time required to pronounce with ease, one vowel, is called one *Mátrá*; that required to pronounce two vowels is called two *Mátrás*; and that required to pronounce three vowels, three *Mátrás*. But the Authorities in Music have held this rule to be unsuited to the requirements of Music; as the duration fixed thereby is too small to bring instrumental accompaniment within its scope, they have accordingly decided that the time required to pronounce five short letters of the alphabet, should be considered the duration of one *Mátrá*.

Q.—What is called the *Laya*?

A.—The uninterrupted flow of the stream of time with reference to the *Hrasva*, *Dírgha*, *Plúta*, *Ardha* and *Anu Mátrás* is called *Laya*. There are three kinds of its course, *viz.*, *Druta* (quick movement), *Madhya* (medium movement) and *Bilamvita* (slow movement.)

Q.—What is the difference between the *Mátrá* and the *Laya*?

A.—The *Mátrá* has no *Chhandah* (or regular Metre) but *Laya* has; without *Chhandah* there can be no *Laya*. *Laya* cannot be determined by one species of *Mátrá*; but it is derived from divisions into metre made by the action of two or more species of *Mátrás*.

For instance :—*Dhá-Tri-Ket*, represents a

Laya; it being made up of one *Mátrá* and two half *Matrás* $(1, \frac{1}{2}, \frac{1}{2})$.

Q—In what way can three *Mátrás* be divided into nine parts?

A.—By eight quarter *Mátrás* and one full *Mátrá*.

Q.—What is called *Chhandah*?

A.—*Chhandah* (metre) means the reduction of the eternal "Time" into *Mátrá* and *Laya*, bringing their diversified course to a narrow compass.

Q.—Why is not *Laya* determined by one *Mátrá* or one species of it?

A.—*Laya* (with sura) pervades the whole universe; it is beyond the comprehension of man to understand and determine it; consequently he seeks by conventional methods to bring *Laya* within a finite scope or range, in order to determine it, which he does by assuming *Laya* to be of a small magnitude. The *Madhya* (medium), *Druta* (quick) and *Bilamvita* (slow) are the three artificial divisions of infinite time which he makes. Taking one of the aforesaid movements, if he repeats by itself again and again, for instance, the phrase Dhá-A, every time in one *Mátra Kála* (or quantity of time), as represented by one small bar, he finds that there is a sameness in the flow of time, and that there is no measure formed out of it; but if he repeats them in conjunction with two or more *Mátrás*, so as to give it the appearance of a metre, such as :—Dhádit Dhá Dhenná, then he is able to determine the *Laya* of this short phrase. Herein lies the difference between the *Mátrá* and the *Laya*.

Q.—What is called *Tála* and how is the derivation of the term explained in the Sañskrit work *Sañgita Darpana*?

A.—The sound that is produced by striking the palm of one hand against that of the other, is called *Tála*. The term is derived from "*Tá*" (the emblematical representation of *Mahádeva*) and "*La*" (the emblematical representation of *Bhagavatí*). The union of *Mahádeva* and his consort *Bhagavatí* (as represented in these two letters) is symbolized in the term *Tála*.

Q.—What are the principal elementary *Bols* (conventional syllables) denoting the beating of time, that should be learned by the student?

A.—*Tá*, *Dit*, *Thun* and *Ná*. These are the four principal sounds that are imitated on pulsatile instruments, which are played to represent rhythmic measure.

Q.—What is the object of giving *Tála* to a song?

A.—To bring out, in a clear manner, the metre to which the song is composed.

Q.—What is the difference between the *Tála* and the *Chhandah*?

A.—The *Tála* is only *Chhandah* in another shape. The *Tála* is subordinate to the *Chhandah*, and is its outward indication.

Q.—Like the other *Chhandahs*, into how many *Pádas* is the *Tála* divided and what is each of them called?

A.—*Tála* has four *Pádas* or divisions, *viz.*,—*Sama*, *Atíta*, *Bishama* and *Anágata*. According to the Musicians, *Tála* or the beats of time, may be commenced from any of these four *Pádas*; hence each is called a *Graha*.

Q.—What are the indications of the aforesaid four *Pádas*?

A.—When *Tála* is beat simultaneously with the commencement of a song, the action is called *Sama Graha*; when *Tála* is beat immediately after the song has been begun, it is called *Atíta Graha*; when the song is commenced after the *Tála* had been beat, it is known as the *Anágata Graha* and when *Tála* is beat half way between the intervals of *Atíta Graha* and *Anágata Graha*, it is termed the *Bishama Graha*.

Q.—What is meant by the word *Sañgata* or *Theká*?

A.—Playing on any pulsatile instrument, as a rhythmic accompaniment to vocal or instrumental music, is called *Sañgata* or, in the language of the Mahomedans, *Theká*.

Q.—What is the object of the *Sañgata* ?

A.—To add to the sweetness of the Music sung or played. It is absolutely necessary for the Student of Music, to practice the *Tála* well, for without *Tála*, say the Authorities on the subject, Music is as insipid as a course of dishes cooked without salt.

Q.—What are the essentials of the *Tála* and what are the signs for expressing them ?

Ághdta (Beat) and *Birâma* (Rest) are the essentials of the *Tála*. The symbol for the former is (↘ or 1) or the numerical figure *one*, and that for the latter is (o) or *nought*. The sign for *Sama* (accent) is (+) or the *Patanga*. All these signs are placed above the symbols which represent the *Mátrás*.

Q.—What is called *Yati* and what is its sign and how is a full *Mátrá* formed ?

A.—The *Yati* or the short rest between *Mátrás* marks out, by its position in the *Tála*, the point of the difference of that *Tála* with another *Tála*, made up of a similar number of *Mátrás*. The *Ághdta* (Beat) together with the *Yati*, make up the complement of a full *Mátrá*. The symbol for *Yati* is thus, *ó* (a nought with a small slanting dash over it). This symbol is placed over the signs which represent the *Mátrás.*

Q.—Into how many kinds are the *Thekás* classified ?

A.—Five ; *viz* :—*Sama, Sarit, Gopuchchha, Pipíliká* and *Mridañga.*

Q.—How many *Pránas* (*Prána* means animate existence, vitality) the *Tála* is said to have and what are they ?

A.—Ten, namely ; *Kála, Márga, Kriyá, Añga, Girá, Játa, Kalá, Laya, Jita and Prasna.*

Q.—How many in number and what are the characteristic qualities of the *Tála* ?

A.—Four ; *viz.,*—*Sama, Atíta, Bishama* and *Anágata.* As the power of consuming is the natural characteristic of Fire, so these four qualities are the outcome of the essential energy of *Tála.*

Q.—What is the difference between *Karttavya* and *Prakromaniká* (otherwise called *Parama*) ?

A.—As the enlargement of a *Gíta* by means of the extension of the various notes of its *Rága*, in accordance with the laws of *Gamaka* and *Múrchchhana*, and with a variety of *Mátrás* is called *Karttavya* or *Karttab ;* so the extension of a *Tála* by expressing a variety of sounds, in varied metres, on the pulsatile instruments, with strict attention to the particular *Laya* which that *Tála* represents, is called *Prakramaniká* or *Parama.*

Q.—Of how many *Mátrás* is *Chautála* formed and how is this *Tála* played on a pulsatile instrument?

A.—*Chautála* is formed of six *Mátrás* of which, four represent *Ághátas* (Beats) and two represent *Súnyas* (Rests); the following table gives the order of the six *Mátrás*, together with their *Yatis*, and the conventional words that are expressed on the pulsatile instruments:

<table>
<tr><td>+
|</td><td>/
o</td><td>o
|</td><td>/
o</td><td>ˎ
|</td><td>/
o</td><td>o
|</td><td>/
o</td></tr>
<tr><td>Dhá</td><td>Dhá</td><td>Dhin</td><td>Tá</td><td>Kóth</td><td>Tágé</td><td>Dhin</td><td>Tá</td></tr>
<tr><td>ˎ
|</td><td>/
o</td><td>ˎ
|</td><td>/
o</td><td></td><td></td><td></td><td></td></tr>
<tr><td>Tete</td><td>Kete</td><td>Gedá</td><td>Ghene</td><td></td><td></td><td></td><td></td></tr>
</table>

CHAPTER IV.

On the *Saptaka, Gráma, Múrchchhaná, Gamaka, Anuloma and Biloma, Bikshepa and Praksepa, &c.*

Q.—What is called a *Saptaka* and how many *Saptakas* are produced by the organism of the human voice?

A.—The aggregate or serial collection of *Sharja* and the other six notes, is called the *Saptaka* (or Septime). The human voice is capable of producing only three *Saptakas.*

Q.—How many *Saptakas* have been recognized in the *Sáma Veda* ?

A.—Since more than three *Saptakas* are not naturally produced by the vocal organism of man, only three *Saptakas* have been mentioned in the *Sáma Veda*. These are :—*Mandra, Madhya* and *Tára ;* or, as they are otherwise called *Anudátta, Sarit* and *Udátta*. The *Anudátta* or *Udárá* (symbol letter *u*) is produced from the navel; the *Sarit* or *Mudárá* (symbol letter *mu*) from the throat and the *Udátta* or *Tárá* (symbol letter *Tá*) from the head. Roughly speaking, the *Udárá, Mudárá* or *Tárá*, represent respectively the lower, middle and higher Septimes.

Q.—What is called the *Swaragráma* ?

A.—The Scale or arrangement of the seven notes, with regard to their proper position in the Septime, is called the *Swaragráma*.

Q.—What are the opinions of the Musical Authorities regarding the construction of the *Gráma ?*

A.—Some Authorities are of opinion that *Sharja* (C), *Gándhára* (E) and *Madhyama* (F) as the three *Grámas* (key notes or tonicks), while others hold that each *Sharja* (C) of the three *Saptakas* is the *Gráma*. The latter opinion seems reasonable, for the position of the other six notes connot be determined without the *Sharja* (C); unless a certain note is fixed as the tonick, every note, in the Septime, is liable to be taken as such.

Q.—Wherein lies the difference between the European and the Sañskrita systems of scales?

A.—The notes being divided into minute divisions of flats and sharps, each such division or *Sruti* can be made to take the place of a key note. The European scale of notes differs from the sañskrita scale in the disposition of the *Srutis.* The Europeans do not recognize minuter intervals than flats and sharps; consequently, their scales are formed of only the seven natural notes and such sharps and flats, as are recognized by them. The scale in which all the minute intervals of Hindu Music come into play, is called by the Musicians of Europe, the Enharmonic scale. The following represents the Chromatic Scale, (*Vikrita Swaragráma*) or the *Achala Thát* (fixed scale), *i. e.*, one which does not necessitate the shifting of frets in a stringed instrument, when the ordinary sharps and flats are required to be used :—

Sá (C) Ri (D flat) Ri (D) Ga (E flat) Ga (E) Ma (F) Ma (F Sharp)

Pa (G) Dha (A flat) Dha (A) Ni (B flat) Ni (B) Sá (C)

The following repesents the Diatonic Scale or the *Sachal Thát* (moveable scale), *i. e.*, one which necessitates the shifting of frets for producing the sharps and flats as required :—

Sá (C) Ri (D) Ga (E) Ma (F) Pa (G) Dha (A) Ni (B) Sá (C)

Q.—Which of the seven notes of the European scale differs in value from that of the Sañskrit Scale ?

A.—The note *Dhaivata* (A) of the Sañskrit Scale, is higher than the same note of the European scale by only one *Srúti*.

Q.—What is called *Múrchchhaná* and what is its sign ?

A.—*Múrchchhaná* means the uninterrupted gliding of one note into another, in the ascending or descending movement, without suppressing the expression of the intervening *Srútis*. The sign is thus 〰. This undulating line is placed under the notes, beginning with the one with which *Múrchchhaná* commences and ending with the one when it teminates.

Q.—What is the effect of a song sung without the *Múrchchhaná* ?

A.—Without the *Múrchchhaná*, a song loses all its sweetness.

Q.—What is called *Gamaka* and what is its sign ?

A.—*Gamaka* means tremelo or a shake. The shake is caused by the contraction and dilation of the vocal chords when the note, operated upon, is in its way out of the mouth. The sign of *Gamaka* (⁀) is placed above the note to be shaken. Two or more of this sign are placed according to the number of times the note is required to be shaken.

Q.—What are called *Anuloma* and *Biloma*?

A.—The gradual ascension of notes is called *Anuloma* or *Árohana* and the gradual descension is called *Biloma* or *Abarohana.*

Q.—What are called *Bikshepa* and *Prakshepa*?

A.—The terms denote a rapid slur; when after producing a certain note, another is produced, by skipping over two or more immediate notes, in the ascending course, the process is called *Bikshepa*; when this is done in the descending course, the process is called *Prakshepa.* The signs for the *Bikshepa* and *Prakshepa* are respectively ⋙ and ⋘ , and these are placed above the notes which are reached by the slurring process.

Q.—What is called the *Bandhaní* and what is the sign for it?

A.—When two, three or more notes have to be expressed in equal duration of time, the sign of the *Mátrá* is placed on the first note, and the group is put under a ligature or tie, called the *Bandhaní*, which is indicated by a ⌐—¬. If, for instance, the three notes C, D and E have to be expressed in the time of one *Mátrá*, the notes are put thus:—C D E (under a ligature). This indicates that the tune value is collectively one *Mátrá*, and individually for each note $\frac{1}{3}$ of a *Mátrá*. Where four notes are put thus:—C D E F (under a ligature), the collective tune value is one *Mátrá*: but that of each note $\frac{1}{4}$ of a *Mátrá*. Where notes are not brought under a ligature, they have to be expressed according to the time-mark placed over each of them.

Q.—Name all the *Bibhájaka Chinhas* or the dividing signs?

A.—When a *Tála* finishes one of its rounds, the notes under its operation are separated from those under the operation of the next round, by a *Bibhájaka Rekhá* or dividing line, which stands exactly in the position of what is called a "Bar" in European music. When a strain is completed, two such Bars are used, and when a song or piece of music is concluded, the *Padma Chinha* or the Lotus (⁘) is placed at the end.

Q.—What is called *Mancha*?

A.—According to the Sañskrita Authorities, the time beginning with the accent of a certain *Tála* and ending before the beginning of the next accent, is called a complete *Mancha, Ferá* or *Áurdá* is the Hindusthâni equivalent of the term *Mancha.*

CHAPTER V.

MISCELLANEOUS QUESTIONS AND ANSWERS.

Q.—Why is *Tumburá* so called ?

A.—Because the Instrument is the invention of the celestial Musician Tumburu.

Q.—How is the *Tumburá* tuned ?

A.—The second and third strings are tuned in unison and form the *Yuri* (pair) and represent the *Sharja* (C) of the *Mudárá Saptaka* (middle Septime.) The first string is tuned the fifth of the *udárá* (lower Septime) and the fourth the Sharja (C) of the same Septime. The first string is called the *Panchama* (G), and the fourth the *Sharja* or *Khuruj* (of the *Udárá* Septime).

Q.—What do you think of the sound of the *Bányá* ?

A.—The sound of the *Bányá,* (a kind of handdrum, giving a bass sound and played with the left hand) though not attractive in itself, acquires some sweetness when it is played in conjunction with the *Dáhiná* (which is also a handdrum forming the complement of the *Bányá*, gives a sharp sound and is played with the right hand.)

Q.—What is the origin and history of the *Mridañga*?

A.—It is said that in the *Satyayuga* (the golden Age) the Mighty Mahádeva, after having slain in war the powerful and invincible demon *Tripurá*, commenced to dance in celebration of his victory, and surrounded by Indra and the other deities. It was with the object of supplying a rhythmic accompaniment to this dance, that Brahmá invented the *Mridañga*. This instrument was originally made of clay (*mrit*), hence the name *Mridañga*, (or clay-bodied). Certain Authorities assert that *Mridañgas* made of clay, having proved very brittle, they began to be constructed of wood in the *Dvâparayuga*, when *Krishna Líla*, or the pastimes of Krishna took place. In some of the *Puránas*, it is further stated, that Brahmá formed the *Mridañga* out of the soft clay into which the earth had been converted by the blood of the slain demon. The skin of the demon served as cover for the two heads of the instrument; his sinews as the thongs that entwine the instrument and pass up and down, and his bones as the wedges passing under the strips.

Q.—What is the use of the *Mridañga*?

A.—The *Mridañga* is used to beat time to songs, instrumental performances or dancing. Both the right and left hands are employed in playing on this instrument.

Q.—What are called *Ghâts* and how many are they?

A.—Each division of the space on the edge of the right-handed head of the instrument, corresponding with the position of the wedge near the left-handed head, is called a *Ghât*. The *Ghâts* are eight in number.

Q.—Into how many classes are instruments divided?

A.—Four; *viz*:—*Tata* or the stringed class; *Susíra* or the wind class; *Ghana*, or the percussion class, made of metals and *Ánaddha* or the pulsatile class made of skin. The *Ánaddha* instruments are again divided into two classes; namely, *Sabhya* (indoor instruments played in *Sabhás* or drawing-room Assemblies) and *Báhirdvári* (outdoor instruments, such as the *Nahabat* and others which are played in out offices or on particular occasions, such as marriage, &c.)

Q.—How many kinds of the *Ghana* class are there and what are they?

A.—There are two kinds of the *Ghana* class, *viz.*;—

(1) *Anurakta* or that which is played as an accompaniment to some other instrument, as *Kharatáli*, *Mandirá*, *&c.*

(2) *Birakta*, that which is played by itself and independently of any other instrument, as *Kańsára*, *Ghantá*, &c.

Q.—Name some of the Musical Instruments?

A.—*Víná*, *Tumburá*, *Mandirá*, *Bańsí*, *Mridańga*, *&c.*

Q.—Into how many classes are the Musical instruments broadly divided?

A.—Two; *viz*;—*Swatahsiddha* and *Anugatasiddha*. Such instruments as are played by themselves, and not as accompaniments to, nor with the help of, the voice or other instruments, are called *Swatahsiddha*. The *Víná* is an instrument of this description. Such instruments as are played as accompaniments to the voice or to any of the *Swatahsiddha* instruments are called the *Anugatasiddha*. The *Mridańga*, *Mandirá*, &c. are instruments of this description.

Q.—What is called *Tána*?

A.—The word *Tána* is derived from the root "*Tana*," and means the extension or variation of a given *Rága* or Air made in the ascending and descending movements and with the help or *Gamakas* and *Múrchchhanás*.

Q.—What is called *Mána*?

A.—The dexterous graces or flourishes made by the player on drum instruments, conformably to the metre of the *Tála* which is being played, come under the name of *Mána*. The Mahomedan name for *Mána* is *Param.*

Q.—What is called *Swarabinyás* ?

A.—The disposition of notes in a song or instrumental piece is called *Swarabinyás.*

Q.—What is the meaning of *Prastáriká* ?

A.—The continued run of a piece, such as Vedic Chant, is called a *Prastáriká.* In the *Prastáriká,* the piece is not confined to any particular measure.

Q.—What is called *Káku* ?

A.—It means a dissonant note.

Q.—What is called a *Pada* ?

A.—A *Pada* is a short series of *Mátrás* strung to a particular metre. It means a foot or a short phrase.

Q.—What is called *Lágdánta ?*

A.—When a song is sung or a piece played without the interruption of *Srútis,* the effect is called *Lágdánta.* A musical effect approaches the idea of *Lágdánta.*

Q.—How many *Pádas* (Feet) constitute a *Chhandah* (metre) ?

A.—Two or four, according to the nature of the songs.

Q.—What is the effect of a song sung without *Múrchchhanás*?

A.—Without *Múrchchhanás*, the song would lose all its beauty and relish, as there would be breaks in the minute intervals that link one note with another. The *Rágas* would not be clearly executed without them.

Q.—What are called the *Upajas?*

A.—The short variations, *(Tánas)* which the Singer or Performer introduces into a song or instrumental piece, in strict accordance with the rules of the *Rága* he is executing, are called *Upajas.* The *Ásthâyí* should be repeated after each execution of the *Upaja.*

Q.—What is called *Báñ*ta?

A.—The act of dividing a *Rága* into small pieces in the course of singing or playing and rendering them, by way of variation, sometimes on the higher, sometimes on the middle and sometimes on the lower Septime.

Q.—What is called *Dama*?

A.—*Dama* is a variation of time. It means duration on certain notes beyond the time allotted to them; the extra time spent over them being made up by making shorter durations on some other notes.

Q.—What is called *Khama*?

A.—Khama means the short rests that are taken in the course of singing or playing. The *Khama* is otherwise called in Hindi *Pahala* or *Otánámá.*

Q.—What are *Dhrupada, Kheyál, &c.* ?

A.—They are the names of the varieties of vocal music.

Q.—Name some of the different varieties of vocal music ?

A.—Dhrupada, Kheyál, Álápa, Swaragráma, Tap-Khyál, Tappá Chaturañga, Telená, Trivata, Bishnupada, Rágamálá, Ját Gulnaks, Ká-olkálvánà, &c.

Q.—Of how many *Pádas* does the *Dhrupada* consist ?

A.—Four ; namely, *Ásthàyí, Antará, Sanchái* and *Ábhoga.* Sometimes the *Dhrupada* consists of only two *Pádas*, and then it is called *Tuk-Dhrupada.*

Q.—What are the names of the aforesaid four *Pádas* ? and what are the rules of their movements ?

A.—Ásthàyí, which means *Abalambana* (mainstay).

Antará, which means *Madhya* (middle course).

Sanchái, which means *Sañgrahakartá* (consolidator).

Ábhoga, which means *Paripúrnatá* (completion.)

Ásthâyí.—The *Ásthâyí* represents the first strain of a song. It commences with the *Sharja* (*C*) of the *Mudárá* (middle Septime) and rises up, sometimes to *Sharja* (*C*) of *Tárá* (higher Septime) then in its descending course, dwells with some show of skill on some of the notes towards the middle portion of the *Mudárá* Septime, and then coming back, finally takes its rest on the *Sharja* (C) with which it began; sometimes after this, it takes a round to (C) of the higher Septime, and then returns to its resting place.

Antará.—The *Antará* repeats the movements of the *Ásthâyí* by transposing them to the key of the *Madhyama* (F) or *Panchama* (G) of the *Mudárá* (middle Septime). It moves onward to (F) or (G) of the *Tárá* (higher Septime), and then on its return, stops at (C) of the *Mudárá* (middle Septime).

Sanchái.—The movement of *Sanchái* consists in making sometimes the (C), sometimes the (F) and sometimes the (G) of the *Mudárá*, as the key-note. The run is up to (C) of the *Tárá* and ends with (C) of the *Mudárá*.

Ábhoga.—Its movement is very nearly the same as that of the *Antará*.

Q.—How many in number are the systems of Hindu music, and who are their Originators?

A.—There are four systems known. These are named, after their Originators, *Someswara*, *Kallinátha*, *Bharata* and *Hanumanta*. The bulk of *Someswara's* work is procurable; but that of *Hanumanta* is very scarce, as the Mahomedans have destroyed it.

Q.—What are the names of the six *Rágas* according to *Someswara*?

A.—*Srí*, *Vasanta*, *Panchama*, *Bhairava*, *Megha* and *Nattanáráyaṉa*. According to other Authorities, *Hindolá*, *Málava*, *Málakosha*, *&c.*, are classed as *Rágas*.

Q.—What is called *Vádí-Sañyoga* and what are its varieties?

A.—The union of notes of a similar character or value is called *Vádi-Sañyoga*. It is of two kinds; namely, *Swajátíya* (partaking of the same character) and *Bijátíya* (being alien in character.)

The union of the three (Cs,) of the three Septimes, is an instance of the former kind of *Sañyoga* (harmony); that of (C, E and G) is an illustration of the latter kind.

Q.—What is called *Sañyogálankára?*

A.—The unspeakably melodious sound, which is produced by the simultaneous expression of two, three or more notes (that are not inimical to one another) is called in music *Sañyogálankára* or Chord. As the mixture of yellow and blue, produces a different color; namely, green; so the combination of two or three different notes, produces a sound different in character from any of those notes.

Q.—What is the effect of Harmony (as understood in European music) on Hindu music?

A.—The musical embellishment called Harmony, as used in European music, is not indispensable to Indian music. On the other hand, its employment tends to destroy the character of Indian music. The continuation of the tonick, its third, its fifth and its eighth, in either vocal or instrumental music, constitutes Harmony or Chord.

Illustrations of Chords:—

	Tonick.	*Third.*	*Fifth.*	*Eighth.*
1.	Sá (C)	Ga (E)	Pa (G)	Sá (C)
2.	Ri (D)	Ma (F)	Dha (A)	Ri (D)
3.	Ga (E)	Pa (G)	Ni (B)	Ga (E)
4.	Ma (F)	Dha (A)	Sá (C)	Ma (F)
5.	Pa (G)	Ni (B)	Ri (D)	Pa (G)
6.	Dha (A)	Sá (C)	Ga (E)	Dha (A)
7.	Ni (B)	Ri (D)	Ma (F)	Ni (B)

Q.—What do the dots over the notes indicate?

A.—A dot over a note indicates that the note belongs to the *Tárá* (higher Septime), one under a note means that the note belongs to the *Uddárá* (lower Septime), notes having no dots over or under them, belong to the *Mudárá* (middle Septime).

Q.—What is called Melody ?

A.—Melody is a succession of notes so arranged as to give pleasure to the mind. Melody is the life and soul of Hindu *Rágas.*

Q.—How many *Rasas* (Passions or Sentiments) pervade Hindu Music ?

A.—According to *Sañgítaratnávalí* there are eight *Rasas* employed in Hindu Music ; *viz* :—

1. *Śringára* or *Ádi* ... (Erotic).
2. *Víra* ... (Heroic).
3. *Karuná* ... (Pathetic).
4. *Hásya* ... (Comic).
5. *Raudra* ... (Terrible).
6. *Bhayánaka* ... (Fearful).
7. *Bíbhatsa* ... (Disgustful).
8. *Adbhúta* ... (Surprising).

Q.—How many and what are the qualifications of a Vocalist ?

A.—Five ; *viz* :—

1. *Atichaturatá*—(Very great skilfulness).
2. *Bala*—(Strength).
3. *Jnánándita*—(Complacency born of knowledge).
4. *Dhármikatá*—(Religiousness).
5. *Sántachittatá*—(Calmness of temper).

Q.—Mention some of the *Tálas* that accompany the *Dhrupada* ?

A.—*Chautála, Dhámár, Teorá, Jháuptála, Teot, Rúpaka, Mohanatála, Rásatála, Dobáhár, Patatátal, &c.*

Q.—Mention some of the *Tálas* that accompany the *Kheyál* ?

A.—*Káoáli, Ekatálá, Madhyamána, Árá, Khemtá, Árá-Khemtá, Dhimátetálá, Thunri, Postá, Yat, &c.*

Q.—What *Tálas* are formed out of the *Dhámár* ?

A.—The *Jháuptála, Teorá* and *Teot* are formed out of the *Dhámár*.

Q.—From what *Tálas the Yat* and the *Ekatálá* are derived ?

A.—The *Yat* is derived trom *Jháuptála* and the *Ekatálá* from *Chautála*.

Q.—What is called *Báni* ?

A.—*Báni* otherwise called *Chála* or *Dhañ* means style of vocal music.

Q.—How many kinds of *Báni* are there ?

A.—Four; *viz* :—*Khándár, Gauhár,* N*auhár,* and *Dágor*. As the seven notes form the essence of songs; the *Sama, Bishama, Atíta* and *Anágata,* the component parts of *Tála* ; so all songs that are based on the different *Rágas* are subject to the laws of *Báni.*

Q.—What are the laws of the four *Bánis* that govern all songs ?

A.—1. *Khándár Báni* is characterised by the employment of more words and less notes.

2. *Gauhár Báni* is indicated by the use of more notes and less words.

3. *Nauhár Báni* has words and notes in equal portion. In this, the piece may be rendered in double or quardruple or oblique movements of time.

4. *Dágor Báni* has in it the characteristics of the aforesaid three *Bánis.* It is said that this was the favorite *Báni* of the celebrated Singer Haridás Swami. It is possible for one *Rága* to be executed in all the four *Bánis.*

Q.—What are the faults of a Singer that are recognised by the Musical Authorities ?

A.—The following fourteen faults are noticed, and Singers are strictly enjoined to avoid them :— (1) *Lajjá* (Bashfulness), (2) *Bhaya* (Fear), (3) *Aprakásitwa* (want of clearness) in rendering the notes and divisions of time), (4) *Sánunásikatá* (uttering a non-nasal letter through the nose), (5) *Sirah-kampana* or *Mudrádosha* (shaking the head or other parts of the body), (6) *Layasthánabibarjjana* or *Belaya* (breaking the even run of the *Laya*), (7) *Kákuswara* (uttering false notes), (8) *Vikritaswara* (want of smoothness in expression), (9) *Bísráma* (taking rest on a note where rest should not be taken), (10) *Aslilatwa* (making use of obscene or inauspicious words, or words calculated to engender hatred), (11) *Utkatatá* (using such *Rágas* or *Mátrás* as are not easily understood), (12) *Váditá* (interruption of utterance due to coughing, spitting or some other cause), (13) *Byákulatá* (indication of haste) and (14) *Tálahínatá* or *Betálá* (want of adherance to the rules of measure).

Q.—What are the following *Ráginis* composed of :— *Multání*, *Káliñgará*, and *Paraja* ?

A.—*Multání* is derived from the *Ráginis Bhímpalaśri* and *Bároná* ; *Káliñgará* from *Gaúrí*, *Rámkelí*, *Paraja* and *Tribaní* ; *Paraja* from *Vasanta* and *Lalita*.

Q.—Mention some *Ráginis* that are nearly allied to each other, or one another ?

A.—*Gaurí* and *Rámkelí* ; *Desa* and *Surat* ; *Hámvira*, *Sarfarddá*, *Chháyánuta* and *Kámoda*.

CHAPTER VI.

Miscellaneous Questions.

1. What is the difference between *Náda*, *Śruti* and Swara ?

2. What is the relation between the *Śruti* and *Swara*? Illustrate it.

3.—Name the tonick of a Scale which will convert D flat into G?

4. Determine the Diatonic notes of a Scale which has B for its tonick?

5. If the fret D is removed from its proper place on the instrument *Setár*, and put exactly midway between the positions of the frets representing C and D, would the fret D, in its removed position, represent exactly D flat?

6. What is called *Múrchchhaná* and what is its use? Draw out by way of illustration, a short notation, in which the symbol of the *Múrchchhaná* is used?

7. What is called *Ḃelaya*?

8. What is called *Dhrupada*?

9. What is the definition of *Kheyál*?

10. What is the meaning of the word *Rága*? Of how many species are they, and into how many classes is each such species divided?

11. Can a *Dhrupada* be composed in *Rágini Jhijhita-Khámbáj* and set to *Tála Árá-theká*?

12. Point out the difference between *Ektálá* and *Chautála*?

13. Why does a *Gamut* consist of seven notes only, and not more?

14. What is call *Mátrá*? Of how many kinds are they, and what are their indicative signs?

15. If four notes are to be expressed in the time of one *Mátrá,* in what ways can they be noted down?

16. What are called *Bikshepa* and *Prakshepa,* and what are their indicative signs?

17. What is *Gíta* (song) and what is the use of having *Tála* for it?

18. What is the difference between *Telená* and *Chaturañga*?

19. Note down the *Ásthâyí* portion of a song set to *Rága Bhairava* and *Tála Káoálì*?

20. What are the meanings of the divisions *Ásthâyí, Antará, Sañchái* and *Ábhoga*?

21. Whence is the *Swara* produced, and what is the meaning of the term?

22. What is the result of the union of Notes and *Mátrás*?

23. Of Vocal and Instrumental Music, prove which has had a prior existence?

24. Name the tonick of the scale where B takes up the position of F. What is the note which, on being made the tonick, will require all the Chromatic notes to make up the Diatonic Scale?

25. What is the *Srúti*? How many *Srútis* are there in a Septime, and how many, in each of the notes of the Septime?

26. What is called *Anuranana* (Vibration) and what is the minimum number of vibrations necessary to make a Musical Sound?

27. Why cannot there be in the *Vikrita-Swara-Gráma* (Chromatic Scale of Indian Music), such a thing as the *Komala-Madhyama* (F. Flat) or *Komala* (Flat) or *Tivra* (Sharp) *Panchama* (G)?

28. In noting down Music, how are the *Ati-Komala Swara* (very Flat note) and *Ati-Tivra Swara* (very Sharp note) expressed?

29. What is called the *Tála*, of how many kinds are they?

30. What are *Vádi*, *Samvádi*, *Anuvádi* and *Vivádi*?

31. Point out the difference between the *Ráginis* Hámvír and Iman-Kalyána?

LIFE OF MEÁH TÁN SEN.

ONCE on a time, Haridás Swámi, a devotee of Vishnu and a Master of Music, was going to Vrindávana with his disciples. While on his journey, he heard that the town of Bejaya was not far from his way. He entered the town with a view to have a look at it and to take rest there for a few days. He had to pass to the town through a forest, where Tanu Misra used to tend his cows. Observing the party from a distance, Tanu, who wished to make some fun by frightening them, entered into the hollow of a tree, where he awaited their arrival. When Haridás came up with his disciples, Tanu Misra began to growl like a tiger. It is said that at sound of the growl, the animals of the forest took fright and sought means to protect themselves. The bulls, with half chewed grass in their mouths, ran away with upturned tails. The cows, lying on the ground and giving suck to the calves, kicked them out of suck and left the place in breathless hurry. The buffalows jumped out of water and stood in a circle in the field. The herd of buck and doe trotted fast into the adjacent forest. In short, all the animals were frightened and eager to save their lives. The disciples of Haridás Swámi, on hearing the dreadful growl once or twice, and witnessing the confusion among the animals, felt very much afraid; but Haridás was not moved at all. It was impossible, he said to his pupils, that a tiger should come in the day time into that small forest and to the pasture, which was so close to the town of Bejaya. He concluded that the growl was not that of a tiger, but that it emanated from a human being. He dispelled the fear of his disciples with these reasonings and ordered one of them to seek out the man that made the noise. The pupil, who was so ordered, could not altogether extricate himself from fear; though he was satisfied in his mind that the growl did not proceed from a tiger. However, at last, backed up by the encouragement given to him by his master, and through the fear of ridicule at the hands of his fellow pilgrims, he went looking about, and after a diligent search, came across the figure of a man concealed in the hollow of a tree. He climbed on it and gave a slap to Tanu on his back. Tanu had hid there to avoid being struck by the party, in case his tricks were detected; but being thus slapped, he attempted to escape by coming down fast from the tree. The stout-bodied disciple, however, held him by the hand, stopped his progress, and after remonstrating with him, asked him for his name and residence; but as he got no answer, except crying, he took Tanu to his master. On seeing the boy, who was of a shining black color, and wore the sacred thread, Haridás wiped the tears from his eyes affectionately, and consoling him with sweet words, asked him his name, residence, caste, and as to who had growled like a tiger in the forest. The boy, with his head cast down and in faltering tones, gave correct answers to the questions put to him. Haridás Swami, being highly pleased, asked him if he could imitate the cry of any other animal. Tanu said that he had practised all the sounds he heard the animals make. Haridás was surprised to hear this, and expressed a desire to hear him imitate the cries of one or two other animals. Tanu complied with Haridás' request. He was then asked the reason of his wandering about in the forest and looking after the cattle in the pasture, which he explained in full. Haridás felt sorry to hear of the little fellow's low profession and of his father's cruelty towards him, and was moved with compassion towards him. He took the sparkling eyes and the expansive forehead of the boy, as expressions of intelligence on his part, and mentally predicted for him a famous career. It was the firm belief of Haridás that, in consequence of his father's ill treatment, Tanu's education and musical culture had been neglected.

N. B.—Tanu subsequently became a great Singer, and under the name of Meáh Tán Sen, adorned the Court of the Mogul Emperor Akbar.

KRIYÁSIDDHA TAURYATRIKA,

OR

PRACTICAL MUSIC.

KRIYÁSIDDHA TAURYATRIKA,

OR

PRACTICAL MUSIC.

———:0:———

First Exercise.

Second Exercise.

Third Exercise.

Fourth Exercise.

Fifth Exercise.

Sixth Exercise.

Seventh Exercise.

Eighth Exercise.

Ninth Exercise.

Tenth Exercise.

Eleventh Exercise.

Twelfth Exercise.

Thirteenth Exercise.

RÁGA BHAIRABA.

TÁLA—KÁOÁLI.

First Strain.

Second Strain.

RÁGINÍ BHAIRABI.

TÁLA—KÁOÁLI.

First Strain.

Second Strain.

RÁGINÍ HÁMBIRA.

TÁLA—KÁOÁLI.

First Strain.

Second Strain.

RÁGINÍ KÁMODA.

TÁLA—KÁOÁLI.

First Strain.

Second Strain.

RÁGINÍ KALYAN.

TÁLA—KÁOÁLI.

First Strain.

Second Strain.

RÁGINÍ BEHÁG.

TÁLA—KÁOÁLI.

First Strain.

Second Strain.

RÁGA MÁLKOS.

TÁLA—KÁOÁLI.

First Strain.

Second Strain.

RÁGINÍ BÁHÁR.

TÁLA—KÁOÁLI.

First Strain.

Second Strain.

RÁGINÍ RÁMKELI.

TÁLA—KÁOÁLI.

First Strain.

Second Strain.

RÁGINÍ BÉHÁGA.

TÁLA—KÁOÁLI.

First Strain.

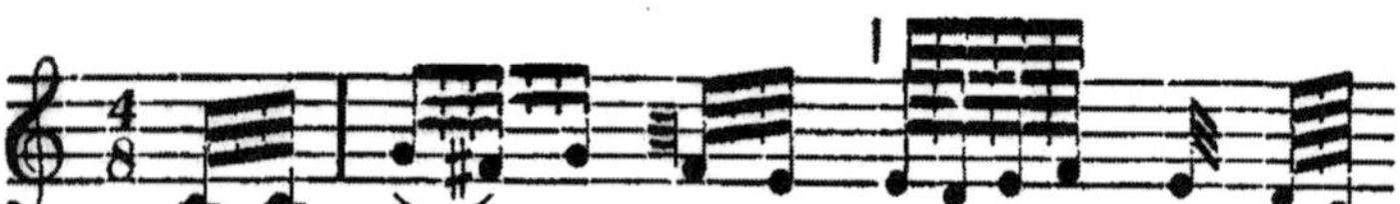

Second Strain.

RÁGINÍ SANKARÁ.

TÁLA—KÁOÁLI.

First Strain.

Second Strain.

RÁGINÍ SANKARÁ.

TÁLA—KÁOÁLI.

First Strain.

Second Strain.

RÁGINÍ LALITA.

TÁLA—ÁRÁTHEKÁ.

First Strain.

Second Strain.

sa ta ta — ni ka te — ba se —
thá ka a ká ra ne — — — bu jhe
chhí — bu jhe chhi á mi svá
bhá bi ka sne ha ba she — — bi
cha ra má sa dá — ká — la san
ta — na sa the á — pa ni —

THE END.

COPIES OF TESTIMONIALS.

21, Kally Persaud Dutt's Street.
Calcutta, 24*th October* 1890.

Baboo MOHINDRA LALL SEAL,
131, *Amherst Street.*

My dear Sir,

With great pleasure I beg to acknowledge receipt of your "Catechism of Hindu Music" in Bengali, and as far as I can make out, it is a very useful book of Music I have ever seen in Bengali; and I trust, without least hesitation, that it will be a first class guide and instructions for those who have even little taste for Hindu Music. With my best regards

I remain
Yours sincerely,
(Sd.) RAMDOSS DASS.
Shashtree.

Bishop's College School,
224, *Lower Circular Road.*
Calcutta, 25th October 1890.

My dear Mr. Seal,

It was most kind of you to send me a copy of your book and I shall value it greatly and not least the excellent Portrait of yourself which appears at the beginning.

Mr. whitehead is at present in England; but your book will be given to him on his return.

Yours very truly,
(Sd.) E. F. BROWN,
Oxford Missionary and Professor.

89, Ripon Street.
Calcutta, 26th October 1890.

Dear Mr. Seal,

I have much pleasure in acknowledging the receipt of your kind present of a copy of your recent treatise on Oriental Music, for which please accept my best and warmest thanks.

With best regards

Believe me,
Yours sincerely,
(Sd.) M. L. SANDEL,
Pleader, High Court.

Calcutta, 30th October 1890.

My dear Mohendro Baboo,

I beg to acknowledge with many thanks your valuable present of a copy of "Catechism of Hindu Music" in Bengali, dedicated to our esteemed friend Raja Sir Sourindro Mohun Tagore, Kt., c. i. e, etc., etc., etc.

The work has been neatly got up. It will be a great help to the Beginners. I will go through the work at my leisure with interest. I wish you every success in your enterprise and you really deserve all praise.

Yours very sincerely,
(Sd.) LOKE NATH GHOSE,
Honorary Registrar, Bengal Music School.

THE PRÁSÁD, "প্রাসাদ"
31st *October* 1890.

MOHINDRO LALL SEAL, ESQUIRE.

DEAR SIR,

Your " Catechism of Hindu Music" is most welcome. Accept my best thanks for the present.

Your labours in the cause of Hindu Music are well-known and ought to be duly appreciated by our countrymen and I have little doubt that continued attention on your part will ensure further improvements.

Yours truly,
(Sd.) JOTEENDRO MOHUN TAGORE, K. C. S. I.

Chupra, 1st *November* 1890.

MY DEAR MR. SEAL,

I am much obliged to you for the little volume on Bengali Music and its theory which you have kindly sent to me. I trust it may help to a more careful training in music specially among our Fellow Christians.

Yours very truly,
(Sd.) P. J. JONES,
Missionary.

ACKNOWLEDGEMENT.

" *Indian Mirror*."—*Dated* 1st *November* 1890.—*Bunga-Shungitar Prosnattur*, or a Catechism of Hindu Music. By Mohindro Lall Seal—Calcutta, 1890.

BETHUNE COLLEGE,
Calcutta, 4*th November* 1890.

MY DEAR SIR,

Many thanks for the Musical Chart and the book which you have so kindly sent me. It is a pleasure to know that gentlemen of our community are devoting their attention to the study of this beautiful Art.

Thanking you again for your kind present,

I remain

Yours truly,

(Sd.) C. M. BOSE, M. A.,

Lady Superintendent.

Calcutta, 5th November 1890.

MY DEAR MOHINDRO BABOO,

I take this opportunity of thanking you most warmly which I should have done much earlier, for the copy of your excellent "Catechism," which you have so kindly presented to me.

I remain

Yours truly,

(Sd.) BAIKUNTHA NATHA BASU,

Honorary Secretary, Bengal Music School.

CHURCH MISSIONARY SOCIETY,

33, Amherst Street,

Calcutta, 6*th November* 1890.

MY DEAR MR. SEAL,

I write to thank you much for kindly sending me a copy of your book. I shall read it with interest and hope it may help me to understand more of Hindu Music.

Yours very truly,

(Sd.) J. W. HALL.

"The Englishman," dated 12th November 1890.

Hindu Music,—Baboo Mohindro Lall Seal, honorary member of the Managing Committee, Bengali Music School, has published a "Catechism of Music" in Bengali, which is a useful addition to this branch of Native literature. In the little book, which is neatly got up, the Author explains the principles of the theoretical and practical music, and the system of notation. It should be a help to students, for it deals with the fundamental principles in a very simple manner. As a frontispiece, we have photograph of the author holding a Tanpura or Native Guitar. It is a good picture, and the musical instrument, one of the most characteristic in India, is well displayed.

32, Chowringhee,
17*th November* 1890.

My dear Sir.

I beg to thank you for your kindness in sending me a copy of your treatise on Hindu Music, which it gives me much pleasure to accept.

Yours truly,
(Sd.) A. W. CROFT, M. A., K. C. I. E.,
Director of Public Instruction, Bengal.

Narikeldanga,
19*th November* 1890.

Dear Sir,

I thank you for your kind present of a copy of your excellent "Catechism of Hindu Music" and of your Chart of Musical Notes. They are no doubt calculated to enlighten our countrymen on a most interesting subject, and they entitle you to the thanks of the public.

Yours truly,
(Sd.) GOOROO DOSS BANNERJEE,
Justice, High Court.

"সহচর।" ১৯শে নবেম্বর ১৮৯০—

বঙ্গ-সঙ্গীতের প্রশ্নোত্তরমালা।—সঙ্গীতবিদ্যাবিশারদ বাবু মহীন্দ্রলাল শীল কর্ত্তৃক প্রণীত। প্রণেতা গ্রন্থখানি রাজা সার সৌরীন্দ্রমোহন ঠাকুরের নামে উৎসর্গীকৃত করিয়াছেন। ৯০ পৃষ্ঠায় গ্রন্থখানি সমাপ্ত হইয়াছে। ইহার কাগজ ভাল, ছাপা সুন্দর, বাঁধাই ইংরাজী ধরণে। ইহাতে গ্রন্থকার সঙ্গীত-শাস্ত্রের গীত, বাদ্য ও নৃত্য, এই তিন কাণ্ডের কথা যথোপযুক্তরূপে আলোচনা করিয়াছেন। গ্রন্থে শেষোক্ত দুইটী কাণ্ড অপেক্ষা গীতের কথা, সমধিক আছে। নাদ, শ্রুতি, স্বর, মাত্রা, লয়, তাল, মূর্চ্ছনা, গমক, অনুলোম ও বিলোমের বিবরণ, বিক্ষেপ ও প্রক্ষেপ সাধন-প্রণালী, ইত্যাদি সকল বিষয়ই সম্যক্‌রূপে বিবৃত ও আলোচিত হইয়াছে। মিঞা তান্‌সেনের জীবনী ও পরিশিষ্টে ক্রিয়াসিদ্ধ তৌর্য্যত্রিক স্বরসাধন-প্রণালী সন্নিবিষ্ট হইয়াছে। আমরা পুস্তকখানি পাঠ করিয়া সঙ্গীত-শাস্ত্রে মহীন্দ্র বাবুর গবেষণার সবিশেষ পরিচয় পাইলাম।

54, Kali Persaud Dutt's Street.
Calcutta, 21*st November* 1890.

My Dear Mr. Seal,

I thank you very much for your kind present of a copy, named "Catechism of Hindu Music," which, I believe, would be a valuable guide to the Beginners, and also to those who have a great desire to study the theoretical parts of the Hindu Music; which is greatly wanting among the common class of our musicians.

Your indefatigable labour in the cause of Hindu Music, will, I hope, draw the attentions of the nobilities in our town and abroad, who are always ready to devote their minds and purse to the encouragement of the musical world. I again accord you my hearty thanks for the present you have so kindly sent to me and best wishes for your improvement to the musical societies.

I am
Yours truly,

(Sd.) DEBENDRA NAUTHA BOSU,
Public Statistician.

Church Missionary Society,
10, Mission Row,
Calcutta, 9th December 1890.

My dear Mr. Seal,

Thank you much for your Catechism of Hindu Music. It was very kind of you to send it me.

With kind regards,

Yours sincerely,
(Sd.) A. CLIFFORD,
Secretary.

Pathuria Ghata Raj Bati,
Calcutta, 18th December, 1890.

My dear Sir,

It is a great pleasure to me to receive your kind present, which you have sent to me just now and I shall preserve the same, considering it most worthy and invaluable production from my good and kind friend's intellect, and I shall be highly glad to let you know gradually as I will go through your work, although I am unacquainted with the music but I am lover of it.

Yours sincerely,
(Sd.) ASHU TOSH CHATTERJEE.

19, Nilmoney Mitter's Street,
Calcutta, 24th February 1891.

My dear Mohindro Babu,

I have a great pleasure in acknowledging the receipt of your palatable present of a copy entitled—" The Catechism of Hindu Music." It has given me not a little pleasure to go through your book, and I make bold to pass this opinion that it is a valuable and scientific addition to works on Hindu Music. May God keep you in sound health and prosper you in the cause of Hindu Music to which you have ably devoted yourself. Herewith I am presenting you my two books on your humble hand. I hope you will go on through these books at your early convenience and encourage me hereafter.

I remain
Yours truly,
(Sd.) BHUBUN KRISHNA MITTER.

LONDON MISSION,
Bhowanipore, 24th February 1891.

DEAR SIR,

I write to thank you for so kindly sending me a copy of your "Catechism of Hindu Music."

I hope it may prove a great help to me and to others.

Yours truly,
(Sd.) L. J. ROBINSON,
Lady Superintendent.

No. 13, GOLUK DUTT'S LANE,
2nd March 1891.

MY DEAR MOHINDRO BABOO,

Accept my best and hearty thanks for the kind present of your "Catechism of Hindu Music."

Your untiring zeal in the cause of Hindu Music deserves every praise and wins for you respects due as an Honorary Member of the Managing Committee of the Bengal Music School.

I have not the smallest doubt that the book is a valuable addition to our musical literature and may be fairly recommended to every lover of this pleasant subject. The clear and simple manner in which the fundamental principles of our Music are dealt with, is calculated to help its readers to a great extent in the way of their learning Hindu Music.

Yours sincerely,
(Sd.) KALLY PROSONNO BANERJEE,
Honorary Superintendent,
BENGAL MUSIC SCHOOL

PRESIDENCY COLLEGE,
Calcutta, 20*th March* 1891.

MY DEAR SIR,

I write to thank you for your kindness in sending me copies of your two books on Hindu Music and for the Musical Chart. The study of Hindu Music has always seemed to me at once most attractive and most difficult. I hope with the aid of your interesting works to gain a clearer insight into the subject.

Yours very truly,
(Sd.) C. R. WILSON,
Professor of Moral and Mental Science.

CITY INSTITUTION,
No. 4, Okhil Mistry's Lane,
Calcutta, 18*th April* 1891.

DEAR SIR,

I have great pleasure to acknowledge with thanks the receipt of your kind present of a copy of your excellent "Catechism of Hindu Music." The work has been neatly got up. It will be a great help to enlighten our countrymen on a most interesting subject. It decidedly entitles you to the thank of the public.

Yours faithfully,
(Sd.) MOTHURA NATH DAS,
Secretary.

C. M. S. BOYS BOARDING SCHOOL,
33, Amherst Street,
Calcutta, 24*th April* 1891.

DEAR MR. SEAL,

Pressure of work has caused the delay in acknowledging your kind gifts.

I am very much interested in Music generally and trust I may, from your Charts, get some insight into native systems of Music.

I think your efforts very praiseworthy, and trust the care and time you have spent in preparing the Charts, may lead many, who are musically inclined, to a careful and systematic study of the science.

I thank you very much for the Charts.

Yours very truly,
(Sd.) FRANK B. GWINN,
Missionary.

8/1, Ram Krishna Bagchee's Lane,
Calcutta, 1*st May* 1891.

Dear Sir,

I have the pleasure to acknowledge receipt of your "Catechism of Hindu Music," in Bengali, which you have kindly presented to me yesterday, and as far as I have gone through it, I deem the book an important treatise for both the beginners and un-theorists. Please accept my best thanks.

Yours truly,
(Sd.) AUBINASH CHUNDER HALDAR,
Student, Bengal Music School.

40, Nyan Chand Dutt's Lane.
Calcutta, the 18*th May* 1891.

Baboo Mohindra Lall Seal.

Dear Sir,

I have much pleasure in receiving the kind present of your "Bungo Sangitar Prosnotter Mala" and my thanks are due to you for it. No doubt it is a valuable present and I appreciate it as such. It will help the Beginners of the Hindu Musical Art a great deal and you will, I hope, not cease in your endeavours to make the treasures of Hindu Music more accessible to the public.

Yours Faithfully,
(Sd.) SUMBOO CHUNDER BANNERJEE.

132, Amherst Street,
Calcutta, 29th June 1891.

M. L. Seal Esquire.

My Dear Sir,

It gives me much pleasure to acknowledge, with thanks, the receipt of a copy of your "Catechism of Hindu Music," a book which clearly shows the amount of labour and energy you have spent to make it interesting and instructive. That the public is under a debt of gratitude to you for your zeal in furthering the study of Hindu Music, I have no doubt.

Very Truly Yours,
(Sd.) SOTISH CHUNDER MITTER.

Beauleah,
21st January 1892.

My Dear Friend,

With the greatest pleasure I accept the nice useful book on music which you have kindly presented me, for which I tender you my best thanks.

With kind compliments,

I remain,
Yours Sincerely,
(Sd.) B. C. CHATTERJEE,
Sub-Judge, Rajshye.

"*The Statesman,*" *dated 2nd August* 1892.—H. H. The Maharaja of Cooch Behar, G. C. I. E., has the honor of presenting to Baboo Mohindra Lall Seal (of 131, Amherst Street, Calcutta), Honorary Member of the Managing Committee, Bengal Music School, Rs. 50, as a complimentary return of the preparation of his music works, which were presented to His Highness. His Highness thus, with his usual spirit of benevolence, has secured encouragement for the Author in the way of furthering his views towards throwing additional light on the subject of the scientific basis of Hindu Music; commending it to the intelligence and taste of European Students of the "Divine Art," and thus to exhibit to many Foreigners, not only the fundamental characteristics of Hindu Music, but also its relation to the European or Western System of Music.

UTTARPARA,
The 30*th August* 1892.

Baboo Mohindra Lall Seal,

DEAR SIR,

I am much obliged to you for the copy of two books and two Charts on Music, which you have kindly presented me. I shall carefully read them and I promise to myself much instruction and pleasure in reading them. The got up both of the books and Charts are better than the ordinary run of Indian productions. I doubt not the matter is even more creditable.

Yours very truly,
(Sd.) RAJAH PEARY MOHUN MOOKERJEE.

9, MOULVY GOLAM SOBHAN'S LANE,
Off Ripon Street,
Calcutta, 12*th September* 1892.

MY DEAR MOHINDRA LAL,

I render most hearty thanks for the splendid presents you have so generously sent me. All of them have been most tastefully and beautifully got up. They reflect very great credit to you. I shall joyfully make the best use of them.

I remain with best wishes,
Ever affectionately yours,
(Sd.) T. C. BANERJEA,
Missionary.

Calcutta, 27th January 1893.

CONSULAT GENERAL.

de France

A' Calcutta.

BABOO M. L. SEAL,

SIR,

I have the honor to inform you that your "Catechism of Hindu Music" has been duly transmitted to the Conservatoire National of Music and of Declamation in Paris, and the Director of this Establishment, in thanking for this despatch, reqested me to convey you the expression of his gratitude and to let you know that the Catechism will be deposited in the library of music and placed at the disposal of the Public.

YOURS FAITHFULLY,

The Consul General for France,

(Sd.) J. JOUSLAIN.

I. C. Bose & Co., Stanhope Press, 249, *Bow-Bazar Street, Calcutta.*